MIAMI
DOLPHINS

BY TONY HUNTER

SportsZone

An Imprint of Abdo Publishing
abdobooks.com

abdobooks.com

Published by Abdo Publishing, a division of ABDO, PO Box 398166, Minneapolis, Minnesota 55439. Copyright © 2019 by Abdo Consulting Group, Inc. International copyrights reserved in all countries. No part of this book may be reproduced in any form without written permission from the publisher. SportsZone™ is a trademark and logo of Abdo Publishing.

Printed in the United States of America, North Mankato, Minnesota
042019
092019

THIS BOOK CONTAINS
RECYCLED MATERIALS

Cover Photo: Tom DiPace/AP Images
Interior Photos: Ben Liebenberg/NFL Photos/AP Images, 4–5, 6, 11, 13, 19, 22, 43; AP Images, 9, 17, 29, 31; Tony Tomsic/AP Images, 21; Kathy Willens/AP Images, 26–27; Gregory Shamus/Getty Images Sport/Getty Images, 34–35; Tim Sharp/AP Images, 36; Wilfredo Lee/AP Images, 39; Aaron M. Sprecher/AP Images, 41

Editor: Patrick Donnelly
Series Designer: Craig Hinton

Library of Congress Control Number: 2018964508

Publisher's Cataloging-in-Publication Data

Names: Hunter, Tony, author.
Title: Miami Dolphins / by Tony Hunter.
Description: Minneapolis, Minnesota : Abdo Publishing, 2020 | Series: Inside the NFL | Includes
    online resources and index.
Identifiers: ISBN 9781532118555 (lib. bdg.) | ISBN 9781532172731 (ebook)
Subjects: LCSH: Miami Dolphins (Football team)--Juvenile literature. | National Football League-
    -Juvenile literature. | Football teams--Juvenile literature. | American football--Juvenile
    literature.
Classification: DDC 796.33264--dc23

TABLE OF
CONTENTS

CHAPTER 1

PERFECTION

The Miami Dolphins had only been around six years when they advanced to Super Bowl VI. But that trip to the big game following the 1971 season turned out to be a forgettable one for the young franchise. The Dallas Cowboys had handed the Dolphins a 24–3 defeat. It was a disappointing ending to a season that once had held such promise.

The 1972 season, however, was shaping up to be one for the record books. The Dolphins had already become the first team to complete a perfect regular season, going 14–0. Then they opened the playoffs with a 20–14 victory over the Cleveland Browns. In the American Football Conference (AFC) Championship Game, they beat the Pittsburgh Steelers 21–17. After 16 games, the Dolphins were still perfect. All they needed now was a victory over Washington in Super Bowl VII.

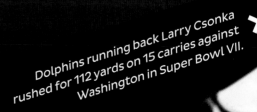

Dolphins running back Larry Csonka rushed for 112 yards on 15 carries against Washington in Super Bowl VII.

Miami quarterback Bob Griese lines up against Washington in Super Bowl VII.

The Dolphins came into the game prepared. Head coach Don Shula had joined the team in 1970. He was already the losing head coach in two of the first six Super Bowls, including the previous one with Miami. This time he made sure his team was ready.

The Dolphins had a consistent offense. In later years, the team would give quarterback Bob Griese more freedom to throw the ball. But in 1972, the Dolphins relied mostly on their running game. The team had three powerful running backs in Larry Csonka, Jim Kiick, and Mercury Morris. Shula liked his team to keep the ball in their hands as much as possible.

The Dolphins wasted no time pounding on Washington. Griese capped a six-play drive with a 28-yard touchdown pass to wide receiver Howard Twilley in the first quarter. Kiick's 1-yard touchdown run in the second quarter extended the lead to 14–0.

Miami held onto that lead through most of the second half. Then, with less than three minutes left, the Dolphins had a chance to put the game out of reach. They brought out kicker Garo Yepremian for a 42-yard field-goal attempt. The Pro Football Hall of Fame later named Yepremian to its 1970s All-Decade team. But he would not make this kick.

Washington's Bill Brundige blocked the attempt. Yepremian picked it up. He attempted to throw a pass, but the ball slipped out of his hand and went straight up in the air. He batted it again, but Washington cornerback Mike Bass pulled it in. Bass took the fumble 49 yards for a touchdown. The Dolphins' lead had been cut to 14–7.

SHULA'S DOMINANCE

In 33 seasons, Don Shula led his teams to a combined 328–156–6 record. No professional head coach had won more games. Those victories extended beyond his 26 years in Miami, where Shula went 257–133–2. He also went 71–23–4 with the Baltimore Colts. Shula took six teams to the Super Bowl (0–1 with the Colts, 2–3 with Miami). He was inducted into the Pro Football Hall of Fame in 1997.

NO NAME? NO PROBLEM!

The Dolphins were known for their "No-Name Defense" during the early 1970s. The defense did not have as many stars as the offense. Still, it helped Miami win four straight division titles starting in 1971. Even though the Dolphins gave up the fewest points and yards in the league in 1972, only two of its defenders—safety Dick Anderson and defensive end Bill Stanfill—earned first-team All-Pro honors. But at least one defender's name will never be lost to history. Safety Jake Scott intercepted two passes against Washington and became the first defensive back to be named the Most Valuable Player (MVP) of a Super Bowl.

"It was a bizarre play. It's hard to believe it could ever happen in a professional football game," Shula said. "It was just such a shock, and I think all of us on the sidelines, when it happened, realized the magnitude of the play, and that the Redskins, who hadn't done anything the whole ballgame, were back with a chance to tie."

The Dolphins got the ball back but had to punt after making only one first down. Washington took over on its own 30-yard line with a little more than a minute left, seven points shy of tying the game.

Now it was up to Miami to hold on. With Super Bowl VII and a perfect season on the line, the "No-Name Defense" held on again. Defensive end Bill Stanfill sacked quarterback Billy Kilmer deep in Washington territory on fourth down to seal the victory.

✕ Don Shula gets a ride off the field after the Dolphins completed their perfect season.

Just like that, Miami had won its first Super Bowl. But perhaps even more importantly, the Dolphins had made history in another way. Until their 1972 season, no team had finished a regular season undefeated and then won the Super Bowl. Now the Dolphins had done so.

"This team is the greatest I have been associated with," Shula said. "It went undefeated and won at the end, and they have to be given credit for their achievement."

CHAPTER 2

MAKING THE DOLPHINS

Joseph Robbie once ran for governor in his native South Dakota. That campaign failed. But Robbie later proved to be a winner to everyone in Miami who loved football.

Robbie graduated from Sisseton High School in 1935. He earned a degree from Northern State College. Then he went on to earn his law degree from the University of South Dakota. That's where Robbie made a friend who proved to be important later in his life.

Robbie moved east to Minneapolis, Minnesota, in 1953. There, he used his talents as an urban planner—someone who helps guide development in a city. He also got involved in football, thanks to his friend from the University of South Dakota.

Bob Griese, shown in 1974, helped the Dolphins break free of their losing ways. He spent 14 seasons in Miami.

MR. STADIUM

Joe Robbie helped fund the construction of Joe Robbie Stadium in Miami. He also served as the national fund-raising chairman for the construction of the DakotaDome in Vermillion, South Dakota. The dome is now home to University of South Dakota football, swimming and diving, and track and field. It also previously was the home of the South Dakota basketball and volleyball teams.

That friend, Joe Foss, was the commissioner of the American Football League (AFL), an upstart rival to the established NFL. In 1965, Robbie traveled to Washington, DC, to meet with Foss, who encouraged Robbie to apply for ownership of an AFL expansion team and, if successful, to place it in Miami.

Robbie visited Miami in May of that year to meet with its mayor, Robert King High. The two talked about whether a new pro team could play in the Orange Bowl stadium. On May 6, 1965, the mayor agreed to invite the AFL to Miami. The AFL agreed to expand for the 1966 season. On August 16, 1965, Joe Robbie and television star Danny Thomas were awarded the Miami expansion team. The price was $7.5 million.

Robbie and Thomas started to build their team through the college draft. Miami selected University of Kentucky quarterback Rick Norton and University of Illinois running back Jim Grabowski in the first round. Neither player panned out.

✗ Joe Robbie, shown in 1970, brought professional football to Miami when he bought the expansion Dolphins in 1965.

Norton went 1–10 as a starter in his four years in Miami. Grabowski opted to play for the Green Bay Packers of the NFL.

The expansion draft took place in January 1966. That allowed the Dolphins to select four players who had been left unprotected from each of the eight existing AFL teams. One of the 32 new players selected was offensive tackle Norm Evans from Houston. He ended up playing 10 seasons with the Dolphins.

Less than three weeks after the AFL expansion draft, George Wilson became the Dolphins' first head coach. Wilson had won four NFL titles as a player with the Chicago Bears and had coached the Detroit Lions before joining Miami. He posted a record of 53–45–6 with the Lions and had won the NFL championship in 1957. His four seasons in Miami were not nearly as successful.

THOMAS ALSO HELPED

Danny Thomas joined Joe Robbie as a founder of the Dolphins. He was also the founder in 1962 of the St. Jude's Children's Research Hospital in Memphis, Tennessee. Thomas was a famous television actor and comedian. He eventually sold his stake in the team to Robbie.

The Dolphins' first season in 1966 ended with a record of 3–11. The 1967 season brought more of the same. However, their 4–10 record did include the debut of a star in the making. In the first game of the season, quarterback John Stofa broke his right ankle. Rookie Bob Griese, Miami's first-round draft pick that year, replaced him. Griese later threw a 68-yard touchdown pass during the Dolphins' 35–21 win over the Denver Broncos at the Orange Bowl.

In November, Griese supplied more fourth-quarter heroics in an exciting win against Buffalo. With 1:01 left, Griese threw a 31-yard touchdown pass to Howard Twilley. That was the game-winning touchdown as Miami won 17–14.

It did not take Griese long to make an impact, even with an average club. During his second year as a pro, Griese threw for 2,473 yards. He also threw 21 touchdown passes. The yardage was a career high. He only topped the touchdown mark once, when he threw 22 in 1977.

NAME THAT TEAM

A fan contest drew 19,843 entries to name the AFL expansion team in Miami. A total of 622 contestants suggested "Dolphins." Joe Robbie said he liked the name because "the dolphin is one of the fastest and smartest creatures in the sea."

Griese offered hope. But four years of poor play were more than enough for the team's fans. Miami's 15–39–2 record in that time span was dismal. Wilson was relieved of his coaching duties following the 1969 season.

One newspaper columnist had an idea for how to stop the losing in Miami. "Why don't you go right to the top and get the best there is? Don Shula."

THE AFL

The AFL was created in 1959 as a rival league to the NFL. When it began play in 1960, few people expected the league to survive. But the league did just that. In fact, by 1966, the AFL and NFL agreed to merge into one league. When the merger was complete in 1970, the 10 AFL teams joined three NFL teams to become today's American Football Conference. The remainder of the NFL teams became today's National Football Conference. Each conference's winner now plays in the Super Bowl.

The AFL began with eight teams, all which remain in today's NFL. They were the Boston (now New England) Patriots, Buffalo Bills, Dallas Texans (Kansas City Chiefs), Denver Broncos, Houston Oilers (Tennessee Titans), Los Angeles Chargers, New York Titans (Jets), and the Oakland (Las Vegas) Raiders. The Dolphins joined the AFL in 1966 and the Cincinnati Bengals became the league's tenth team in 1968.

And that's exactly what Robbie did. Coming off seven consecutive winning seasons and the 1968 NFL title with the Colts, Shula was one of the hottest coaches in the league. His arrival in 1970 brought with it a newfound commitment to success. For Griese, Shula also provided a springboard to his career. That boost eventually helped land Griese in the Pro Football Hall of Fame.

✕ Don Shula was brought in to change the fortunes of the Dolphins. He had guided the Baltimore Colts to seven straight winning seasons.

CHAPTER 3

PRESERVING PERFECTION

Don Shula took over as Miami's head coach in 1970. In the season before, the Dolphins had been a lowly 3–10–1. Shula's first step to success was implementing a new schedule during training camp. It was a drastic change for the players.

Shula scheduled four practices a day. The 7:00 a.m. start included special teams and the kicking game. A 7:45 a.m. breakfast was followed by a 9:30 a.m. meeting to cover the details of that day's upcoming sessions. At 10:00 a.m., the running game (both offense and defense) took priority. Lunch was at 11:30 a.m. Then came another meeting at 3:00 p.m. One half hour later, the passing game (both offense and defense) took center stage. Dinner at 6:00 p.m. was followed by a 7:30 p.m. practice that was used to work on corrections.

Bruising fullback Larry Csonka went to five straight Pro Bowls from 1970 through 1974.

BOB GRIESE

Bob Griese retired in 1980 after spending 14 seasons with the Dolphins. During his career, he played in eight Pro Bowls or AFL All-Star Games. Griese also became the fourteenth passer in football history to throw for more than 25,000 yards in a career. He was inducted into the Pro Football Hall of Fame in 1990. Griese went on to become a sports broadcaster.

This practice lasted until dark. After a 9:30 p.m. meeting, the team was dismissed at 10:30 p.m.

"My players couldn't believe what I was asking them to do," Shula said. "There was a lot of moaning and groaning from the guys. 'Four practices a day!' 'This is unheard of!' 'What's he trying to do? Kill us?'"

Shula was merely preparing the players for the success that lay ahead of them. The Dolphins reached Super Bowl VI after the 1971 season but lost to the Dallas Cowboys. They entered the 1972 season with hopes of taking the next step.

Midway through the perfect 1972 season, however, Miami fans had reason to worry. In Week 5, Bob Griese broke his leg. Earl Morrall, a 38-year-old veteran who had played for Shula in Baltimore, replaced the young superstar at quarterback. Under Shula's guidance, Morrall picked up right where Griese left off, leading the Dolphins to nine more victories. Griese returned

Earl Morrall filled in just fine for the injured Griese during the Dolphins' perfect 1972 season.

late in the season and started the Super Bowl win over Washington, finishing off the amazing 17–0 season.

After their perfect season, the Dolphins' winning streak was snapped in Week 2 of the 1973 schedule. They lost 12–7 to the Raiders in Oakland. Then Miami won its next 10 games, meaning the Dolphins won 28 of 29 games in that span. They returned to the Super Bowl and easily defeated the Minnesota Vikings 24–7 for their second straight championship.

Bob Griese (12) hands off to running back Jim Kiick (21) during a 1971 game against the Rams in Los Angeles.

Csonka was named MVP of Super Bowl VIII. He ran for 145 yards and two touchdowns on 33 carries. Csonka also landed in the Pro Football Hall of Fame after a spectacular career, even though he wasn't playing in a climate well suited to a guy who grew up in northern Ohio.

"When I was playing and practicing in that heat in July and August in Miami with shoulder pads on, it just vaporized me," said Csonka, who later moved to Alaska. "Shula would always come over and look at me and say, 'Where are you? I know you're not here. You're just on automatic pilot.' I was up here [in Alaska] in my mind, fishing in a stream."

The early 1970s was a running era for the Dolphins. The Miami offense had a three-headed monster in the backfield. In 1972 Csonka and Mercury Morris became the first duo in NFL history to each rush for at least 1,000 yards in a season. Teammate Jim Kiick chipped in another 521 rushing yards. The trio led the Dolphins to three straight Super Bowls, ending with Super Bowl VIII after the 1973 season.

In the team's history, the Dolphins have had four games in which two players each rushed for at least 100 yards. Csonka and Kiick accomplished the feat twice, both times in 1971. Morris and Don Nottingham did it against Green Bay in 1975. Morris also excelled as kick returner. In the 1971 season, Morris led the AFC with a 28.2-yard average on kickoff returns.

"ZONK"

Larry Csonka became known as "Zonk" during his time on the Dolphins' three consecutive Super Bowl teams. He ended his career with an average of 4.5 yards per carry and 53 touchdowns as a Dolphin. He rushed for more than 1,000 yards in each of those three Super Bowl seasons. Csonka was a five-time Pro Bowl selection.

Together, the three running backs put up numbers that teammates might never again match. Csonka is the Dolphins' all-time leading rusher with 6,737 career yards. Through 2018, Ricky Williams was second, 301 yards behind Csonka. Ronnie Brown was third, followed by Morris and Kiick.

Meanwhile, the Dolphins' "No-Name Defense" was a fitting nickname for the Super Bowl-bound teams of the 1970s. Linebacker Nick Buoniconti, undersized at 5-feet-11 and 220 pounds, led the group. He also ended up in the Pro Football Hall of Fame. He is the only player from those Dolphins' defenses to achieve such glory.

Over the years, many teams have threatened to join the 1972 Dolphins in their exclusive club. But through 2018, none have finished the job. In 1985 one of the best teams in NFL history came close. But their dreams of perfection crashed on the Orange Bowl turf.

Behind a strong defense, head coach Mike Ditka and the 1985 Chicago Bears looked poised to join the 1972 Dolphins in having a perfect season. Chicago was nearly unstoppable. Buddy Ryan, the Bears' fiery defensive coordinator, had introduced a new defensive scheme that had helped the Bears limit the opposing team to 12.4 points per game.

Then, in Week 13 of the 16-week season, the Bears ran into Miami. The Dolphins were a good team, too. And thanks to the 1972 team, they also had a special motivation to beat Chicago. On *Monday Night Football*, the Dolphins handed the Bears their only loss of the season, 38–24.

"If we hadn't upset them in that Monday-night game, they could have conceivably been an undefeated team—they were that good," Shula said of the '85 Bears. "But we dominated that night, and, again, that makes that accomplishment more important in my reflections of my coaching career."

BUONICONTI A GEM

Linebacker Nick Buoniconti starred at the University of Notre Dame before becoming an NFL legend. Buoniconti has also been a beacon of hope for many people who suffer from spinal cord injuries. In 1985, his son Marc suffered a devastating spinal cord injury. After that, Nick spent much time raising awareness and funds for research into spinal cord injuries. He helped found the Miami Project to Cure Paralysis, which has become known as the world's leading center for spinal cord injuries. On the field, Buoniconti was a star linebacker. He played 14 seasons, including seven with Miami. He was an eight-time All-AFL/AFC selection. Buoniconti was inducted into the Pro Football Hall of Fame in 2001.

CHAPTER 4

A SOLUTION UNDER CENTER

The Dolphins grew spoiled with Bob Griese at quarterback. Year after year for more than a decade, Don Shula knew exactly who would be under center for his team in Week 1. That allowed him and his coaching staff to focus on improving the team at other positions.

In the 1970s, the Dolphins drafted nine quarterbacks, but only one was taken higher than the fourth round. And only two of them ever took a snap for Miami. One of them was Don Strock. A longtime Dolphins backup, Strock was not a superstar, but he was ready when called upon.

One of those times came in January 1982, when Miami hosted the San Diego Chargers in a playoff game at the Orange Bowl. David Woodley, 23, was the youngest

Miami's backup quarterback Don Strock throws a pass in a 1979 game.

AN OVERTIME THRILLER

As he entered the game trailing 24–0 in the AFC playoffs in January 1982, Dolphins quarterback Don Strock did his best to match Chargers star quarterback Dan Fouts completion for completion. One of Strock's passes is among the most memorable plays in team history. With six seconds left in the first half, Strock threw a 15-yard pass to wide receiver Duriel Harris. After catching it, Harris pitched the ball back to running back Tony Nathan. Nathan then ran the last 25 yards for the touchdown. The so-called "hook and lateral" play cut the Chargers' lead to 24–17 at halftime.

Strock only got better as the game went on. In fact, he put up the best numbers of his career. Strock went 29 -for-43 passing for 403 yards and four touchdowns.

Fouts played well, too. It was the first game in NFL history in which both quarterbacks threw for more than 400 yards. The teams were tied after regulation. In overtime, each team missed a field goal. Then San Diego's Rolf Benirschke booted a 29-yard field goal with 1:08 left in overtime for the win. San Diego's 41–38 win was the highest scoring game in playoff history at the time.

quarterback to start a playoff game at the time. But he didn't last long. After the first quarter, Miami was down 24–0. Strock took over for Woodley early in the second quarter. The game took a wild turn as both teams ended up throwing for more than 400 yards. The Chargers won a 41–38 shootout in one of the highest-scoring playoff games in NFL history.

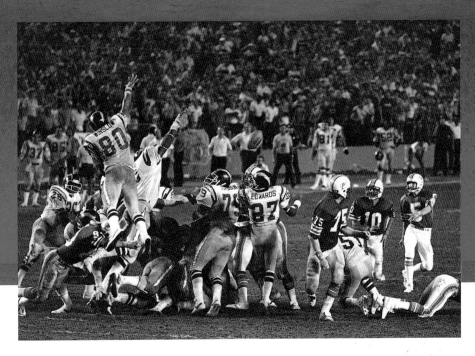

The Chargers block the Dolphins' overtime field-goal attempt in their January 1982 playoff thriller.

The Dolphins rebounded quickly. They returned to the Super Bowl after the 1982 season. However, they ended up losing to Washington 27–17.

Still, knowing that neither Strock nor Woodley was a potential franchise quarterback, Miami used its first-round pick in the 1983 draft to select strong-armed Dan Marino from the University of Pittsburgh. Marino would become one of the greatest quarterbacks in NFL history. But in the 1983 draft, some teams weren't sold on him. When Miami selected Marino with the twenty-seventh pick, five other quarterbacks had already been drafted.

"I'd been hoping Marino would be there, but I didn't see any logical way he could," said Shula, who clearly was not among Marino's doubters. "I'd seen him in the Hula Bowl and [in the] Senior Bowl. All he'd done was win the MVP in both."

Marino replaced Woodley after five games in 1983. He went on to be named NFL Rookie of the Year. Marino then had a record-breaking season in 1984. He shattered NFL records with 48 touchdown passes, 362 completions, and 5,084 passing yards. The previous touchdown record had been only 36 in one season. Marino also became the first quarterback to throw for 5,000 yards in a season.

Marino again looked invincible in the AFC Championship Game after that season, throwing for 421 yards and four touchdowns as the Dolphins cruised past the Pittsburgh Steelers. Fans were eager to see what he would do against the San Francisco 49ers in Super Bowl XIX.

✕ Rookie quarterback Dan Marino looks for a receiver during a playoff game against the Seattle Seahawks in December 1983.

Marino had reached the Super Bowl after only his second season. But his hot streak ran out in the season's final game. He threw 50 passes but connected for only one touchdown. It was an otherwise forgettable game for Dolphins fans.

Miami lost 38–16 to the 49ers and their own star quarterback, Joe Montana. After Marino's successful season, Dolphins fans figured it was only a matter of time before they were once again regulars at the Super Bowl. But Marino and the Dolphins never made it back to the Super Bowl. He did continue to set new records, however. One that Marino was particularly proud of was his streak of consecutive starts—145, the most ever by a quarterback at the time.

Marino created many memorable plays with his accurate passing. One became known as the "Clock Play." In a 1994 game, the Dolphins trailed the New York Jets by 18 points on the road. Marino led Miami on an epic comeback. With less than 30 seconds left and the clock running, Miami had the ball on the Jets' 8-yard line. The Dolphins were trailing 24–21. Since they were out of timeouts, most people expected Marino to spike the ball and stop the clock. That would give the Dolphins time to send out the kicking team to try for a potential game-tying field goal.

Marino signaled that he was going to spike the ball to stop the clock. But it was a decoy. Instead, Marino took the snap and dropped back to pass. He hit wide receiver Mark Ingram in the end zone. It was Ingram's fourth touchdown of the game. The Dolphins won 28–24.

A MAJOR TALENT

Dan Marino was one of the most feared players in the NFL. "He's a phenom," Buffalo defensive end Bruce Smith told *Sports Illustrated* in 1996. "There couldn't have been a better passer ever. I mean, the guy just doesn't miss. And he's not fast, but you can't catch him. Playing him twice a year is like playing [New York Yankees great Joe] DiMaggio all the time."

Even Marino said that he sometimes felt unstoppable. "There were times on the field when I felt like I couldn't miss," Marino said. "The ball was always on time, it was always catchable, and I was making the right decisions on who to throw to."

The teams that passed on drafting Marino were kicking themselves later. The quarterback was selected to nine Pro Bowls during his career and left Miami with dozens of offensive records. He was enshrined in the Pro Football Hall of Fame in 2005.

Shula retired after the 1995 season. New coach Jimmy Johnson helped guide Miami to the playoffs in three of the next four seasons. But after the 1999 season, Marino was 38 years old. After leading the Dolphins to a 147–93 record in 17 seasons as the starting quarterback, he decided to retire. Once again the Dolphins needed a new quarterback. They decided to take a whole new approach to the game as well.

CHAPTER 5

PIVOT TO
DEFENSE

With the high-scoring Marino Era over, the Dolphins returned to their roots and leaned hard on their defense, led by middle linebacker Zach Thomas. He was a five-time All-Pro first-team pick who controlled the field for Miami from 1996 to 2007.

Defensive end Jason Taylor was another dominant defender who became a fan favorite in Miami. Standing 6-foot-6 with the speed of an outside linebacker, he was bad news for opposing offenses. In 2000 Taylor was named first-team All-Pro after posting 14.5 sacks. Two years later, he led the league with a career-high 18.5 sacks. It was part of an eight-year span in which he averaged 12.5 sacks per season.

Jason Taylor (99) and Zach Thomas (54) were the fearsome leaders of the Dolphins defense.

Head coach Dave Wannstedt led the Dolphins to the playoffs in 2000 and 2001.

The new emphasis on defense came into focus when former Bears head coach Dave Wannstedt took over the Dolphins in 2000. In three of his first four seasons in Miami, Wannstedt's defenses finished in the top four in the NFL in fewest points allowed. The Dolphins went 11–5 in 2000 and 2001, and they reached the playoffs both seasons.

Miami finished the next two seasons above .500 as well but didn't reach the postseason. Then Wannstedt was let go after a 1–8 start to the 2004 season.

The Dolphins swung for the fences with their next coach in bringing in Nick Saban, who had coached Louisiana State University to a share of the national title in 2003. Saban had spent six seasons as an NFL assistant but hadn't been on a professional sideline in a decade. It turned out his style was better suited to the college game. The Dolphins went 9–7 and 6–10 in two seasons under Saban, who went on to an unprecedented stretch of success at the University of Alabama.

Miami then turned to former Indiana University head coach and San Diego Chargers offensive coordinator Cam Cameron. That decision was a resounding failure.

Cameron's one year as head coach in 2007 produced a 1–15 record. The 2007 Dolphins lost their first 13 games, six of them by three points. They appeared to be headed to 0–14 with another heartbreaking loss against the Baltimore Ravens. Tied 16–16 in overtime, Baltimore's usually steady kicker, Matt Stover, lined up for a game-winning

BOUNCE-BACK SEASON

After their dismal 1–15 showing in 2007, Miami rebounded in a big way. The Dolphins won the AFC East in 2008 behind the efficient play of quarterback Chad Pennington and the dynamic running of Ronnie Brown. Linebacker Joey Porter was the only Pro Bowler on a new no-name defense that forced 30 turnovers.

A WILD IDEA

Tony Sparano wanted to make an impact in his first season as Miami Dolphins head coach. He did just that early in 2008. After scoring only 24 points in their first two games—both losses—Sparano pulled the trigger on the Wildcat formation. In the Wildcat, quarterback Chad Pennington split wide and running back Ronnie Brown took a shotgun snap. Brown then had the option to run or pass. The Wildcat was a huge success when Sparano rolled it out at New England in Week 3. Brown ran for four touchdowns and threw a 19-yard touchdown pass as Miami rolled to a 38–13 win. The Patriots had no answer for the Wildcat, and soon the other NFL teams were working on their own versions of the formation.

44-yard field goal. But he missed! Three plays later, Dolphins quarterback Cleo Lemon hit receiver Greg Camarillo with a short pass at midfield. Camarillo found a seam in the defense and outran the Ravens to the end zone. The 22–16 victory was Miami's only win of the season.

Things began to turn around in December 2007. Owner Wayne Huizenga, who had purchased the team in 1994, hired Bill Parcells as the team's executive vice president of football operations. Parcells had won two Super Bowls as a head coach of the New York Giants. He'd also had success in the AFC East, leading the Patriots to the Super Bowl and the Jets to the AFC Championship Game. His first move was to hire former Dallas Cowboys assistant head coach Tony Sparano to run the show in Miami.

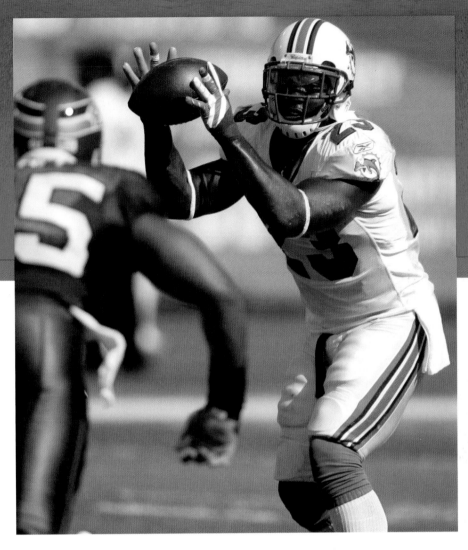

Dolphins running back Ronnie Brown takes the snap in the Wildcat formation.

The Dolphins went 11–5 and won the division in 2008, snapping New England's five-year stranglehold on the AFC East. Their success was in part due to their effective use of the Wildcat formation, in which the ball is snapped directly to the running back. But the Dolphins were back below .500 the next three seasons, and Sparano was out in 2011.

Miami entered 2012 still looking for a quarterback who could play anywhere near the caliber of Marino. With new head coach Joe Philbin in place, the Dolphins took quarterback Ryan Tannehill from Texas A&M with the eighth overall pick in the 2012 NFL Draft. Tannehill wasn't a big name, but he had impressed NFL scouts with the throws he made in college. It helped that he was going to learn under Philbin, who had worked with Aaron Rodgers when Philbin was Green Bay's offensive coordinator.

Tannehill kept Miami right around .500 in his first four years. But the Dolphins just could not get into the playoffs. This eventually led to Philbin being fired in 2015 when the team started 1–3.

Once again, Miami went with another offense-minded coach in Adam Gase for the 2016 season. This time, it worked out for the Dolphins. With Tannehill at quarterback, Miami broke its seven-year playoff drought. The Dolphins went 10–6 but were eliminated in the wild-card round of the playoffs.

Miami looked to have some momentum after its playoff appearance in 2016, but it was derailed before the next

Quarterback Ryan Tannehill was back in 2018 as the Dolphins looked to once again challenge for the AFC East crown.

season even started when Tannehill tore the ACL in his left knee in training camp. He returned in 2018 looking to find the chemistry that he and Gase had shown in their promising first season together.

Instead, the Dolphins wasted a 3–0 start and lost their last three games to finish 7–9. Gase was fired after the season and replaced by former New England defensive coordinator Brian Flores. The Dolphins also traded Tannehill to the Tennessee Titans. With a new head coach and a new quarterback coming in, the Dolphins looked at 2019 as the start of a new future in Miami.

TIMELINE

Minneapolis lawyer Joe Robbie meets with Joe Foss in Washington, DC, on March 3. The AFL commissioner advises Robbie to apply for an expansion franchise in Miami.

On August 16, the AFL awards its first expansion franchise to Robbie and television star Danny Thomas for $7.5 million.

The Dolphins defeat Denver 24–7 on October 16 for the first win in franchise history. That ends a string of nine losses, including four in the preseason.

After seven years as coach of the Baltimore Colts, Don Shula becomes head coach and vice president of the Dolphins on February 18.

The Dallas Cowboys defeat Miami 24–3 in Super Bowl VI on January 16 in New Orleans, Louisiana.

1965

1965

1966

1970

1972

The Dolphins go 14–0 in the regular season. On January 14, 1973, the Dolphins cap a perfect 17–0 season by winning Super Bowl VII 14–7 over Washington.

The Dolphins win their second Super Bowl in a row with a 24–7 win over the Minnesota Vikings on January 13. Larry Csonka gains 145 yards rushing on his way to being named MVP.

Bob Griese retires on June 25 after a 14-year career with the Dolphins. The six-time Pro Bowl selection guided the Dolphins to two Super Bowl victories.

Don Strock brings the Dolphins back from a 24–0 deficit, only to see Miami lose 41–38 in overtime to the San Diego Chargers on January 2.

Playing in their fourth Super Bowl, the Dolphins fall to Washington 27–17 on January 30.

1972

1974

1981

1982

1983

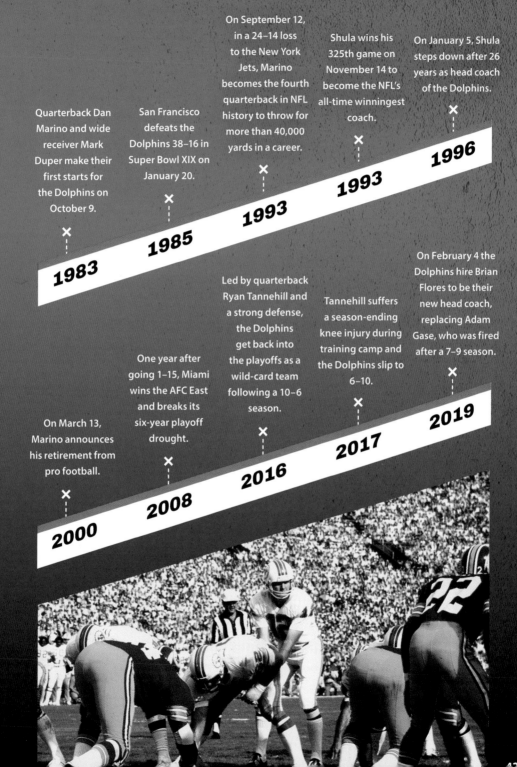

Quarterback Dan Marino and wide receiver Mark Duper make their first starts for the Dolphins on October 9.

1983

San Francisco defeats the Dolphins 38–16 in Super Bowl XIX on January 20.

1985

On September 12, in a 24–14 loss to the New York Jets, Marino becomes the fourth quarterback in NFL history to throw for more than 40,000 yards in a career.

1993

Shula wins his 325th game on November 14 to become the NFL's all-time winningest coach.

1993

On January 5, Shula steps down after 26 years as head coach of the Dolphins.

1996

On March 13, Marino announces his retirement from pro football.

2000

One year after going 1–15, Miami wins the AFC East and breaks its six-year playoff drought.

2008

Led by quarterback Ryan Tannehill and a strong defense, the Dolphins get back into the playoffs as a wild-card team following a 10–6 season.

2016

Tannehill suffers a season-ending knee injury during training camp and the Dolphins slip to 6–10.

2017

On February 4 the Dolphins hire Brian Flores to be their new head coach, replacing Adam Gase, who was fired after a 7–9 season.

2019

QUICK STATS

FRANCHISE HISTORY

1966–69 (AFL)
1970– (NFL)

SUPER BOWLS
(wins in bold)

1971 (VI), **1972 (VII)**, **1973 (VIII)**, 1982 (XVII), 1984 (XIX)

AFC CHAMPIONSHIP GAMES *(since 1970 AFL-NFL merger)*

1971, 1972, 1973, 1982, 1984, 1985, 1992

DIVISION CHAMPIONSHIPS *(since 1970 AFL-NFL merger)*

1971, 1972, 1973, 1974, 1979, 1981, 1983, 1984, 1985, 1992, 1994, 2000, 2008

KEY COACHES

Jimmy Johnson (1996–99): 36–28, 2–3 (playoffs)
Don Shula (1970–95): 257–133–2, 17–14 (playoffs)

KEY PLAYERS *(positions, seasons with team)*

Nick Buoniconti (LB, 1969–76)
Mark Clayton (WR, 1983–92)
Larry Csonka (FB, 1968–74, 1979)
Bob Griese (QB, 1967–80)
Bob Kuechenberg (G, 1970–83)
Jim Langer (C, 1970–79)
Larry Little (G, 1969–80)
Dan Marino (QB, 1983–99)
Mercury Morris (RB, 1969–75)
Dwight Stephenson (C, 1980–87)
Jason Taylor (DE, 1997–2007, 2009, 2011)
Zach Thomas (LB, 1996–2007)
Richmond Webb (T, 1990–2000)
Ricky Williams (RB, 2002–03, 2005, 2007–10)

HOME FIELDS

Hard Rock Stadium (1987–)
Also known as Joe Robbie Stadium, Pro Player Park, Pro Player Stadium, Dolphins Stadium, Dolphin Stadium, Sun Life Stadium, New Miami Stadium, and Land Shark Stadium.
Orange Bowl (1966–86)

QUOTES AND ANECDOTES

"The thing that stands out about the Super Bowl was that we were 16–0, going to the Super Bowl against the Washington Redskins, the only team that has ever gotten that far. We were underdogs—16–0, and we were underdogs in the Super Bowl. That just told us that we'd won all these games, but we weren't getting any respect from somebody."

—Bob Griese on Super Bowl VII, which capped Miami's perfect 1972 season

Garo Yepremian kicked a field goal to give the Dolphins a victory over the Kansas City Chiefs on December 25, 1971. But by the time he took the field, fans were starting to wonder if the game would ever end. The teams used 82 minutes and 40 seconds of game time—the longest game in NFL history—to decide the outcome. Yepremian scored a league-high 905 points in the 1970s.

In 1996, there were 18 quarterbacks in the Pro Football Hall of Fame. In Dan Marino's first 10 seasons in the league, he threw for at least 12,000 more yards than any of those 18 had in their first 10 seasons.

"It was always banging into things, knocking things over, and he was the kind of dog [that] if he ran away, I knew he would come back."

—Don Shula, on why he named his collie puppy "Zonk," Larry Csonka's nickname

Miami played in the Orange Bowl for 21 years before moving into its current home. Since the Dolphins moved in 1987, their home stadium has had 10 different names and two different timespans in which the stadium was called Dolphin Stadium. The most recent name, Hard Rock Stadium, was adopted in August 2016.

GLOSSARY

draft
A system that allows teams to acquire new players coming into a league.

expansion
The addition of new teams to increase the size of a league.

hall of fame
A place built to honor noteworthy achievements by athletes in their respective sports.

legend
A person who achieves fame.

paralysis
The inability to move a body part.

rookie
A professional athlete in his or her first year of competition.

snap
The start of each play, when the center hikes the ball between his legs to a player behind him, usually the quarterback.

spike
The act of throwing the ball to the ground to stop the clock.

MORE INFORMATION

BOOKS

Cohn, Nate. *Miami Dolphins*. New York: AV2 by Weigl, 2018.

Graves, Will. *The Best NFL Offenses of All Time*. Minneapolis, MN: Abdo Publishing, 2014.

Myers, Dan. *Miami Dolphins*. Minneapolis, MN: Abdo Publishing, 2017.

ONLINE RESOURCES

To learn more about the Miami Dolphins, visit **abdobooklinks.com** or scan this QR code. These links are routinely monitored and updated to provide the most current information available.

PLACE TO VISIT

Hard Rock Stadium
347 Don Shula Dr.
Miami Gardens, FL 33056
305–943–8000
hardrockstadium.com

This stadium has been the home of the Dolphins since 1987. Five Super Bowls were held there between 1989 and 2010. It also hosts University of Miami football games.

INDEX

ABOUT THE AUTHOR

Tony Hunter is a writer from Castle Rock, Colorado. This is his first children's book series. He lives with his daughter and his trusty Rottweiler, Dan.